Beyond the Rainbow

The Truly Amazing Story of
Rosemary and Nicola Spencer

"Nicola went into what appeared to be a trance, suddenly messages from her dead Father streamed from the pen. Contact had been made."

Written by Rosemary Spencer
through the mediumship of
Nicola Spencer

Edited by Alan Pemberton

This book includes dramatic revelations from Lady Diana, speaking from the world of spirit

First published in Great Britain by
Pen Press Publishers Ltd
39-41, North Road
Islington
London N7 9DP

ISBN 1-905203-44-6

Printed and bound in the UK

A catalogue record of this book is available from
the British Library

Front cover design; Rosemary Spencer
Painting of Lady Diana; Peter Robinson
Poetry; Alan Pemberton

Beyond the Rainbow

Written by Rosemary Spencer
Through the mediumship of
Nicola Spencer

Edited by Alan Pemberton

This book is dedicated to Nicola's mother Jean
and her grandchildren

This book would not have been possible without the help of my
stepdaughter, Nicola Spencer, and the discovery of her
mediumistic abilities following the death of her father. I am also
grateful to my friend the writer, Alan Pemberton, who helped me so
much with the editing of this manuscript. A selection of his
beautiful poems appears throughout this book.

Many of the world's religions promise resurrection but it is rare
indeed to actually receive direct communication from a loved one
who has passed on giving us first hand evidence of their
experience in the promised land.

Introduction

Before my first husband Dennis, passed over following a long period of poor health, we both attended a Spiritualist Church. He was a very spiritual man who believed firmly in an afterlife.

A few weeks after his death I was impressed to go to a medium - as so many of us are following bereavement. The medium told me that she had my husband with her and that he was introducing a dark haired man. He was showing me a ring, which was being placed on my finger with his blessing.

Within a year of Dennis's passing I had moved to Bournemouth from Weymouth. I attended the local Spiritualist Church (Bath Road) where I met the dark haired man, fell in love and we were soon married. His name was Don, the subject of this book.

When we first met and began talking we discovered that our previous partners, Jean and Dennis, died on the same day of the same month of the same year. Both had died from the same condition – there are no coincidences!

Sadly, after seven happy years together, Don died following a year of ill health.

Don had become a spiritualist following the death of his first wife, Jean; he was also a healer and a man who passionately furthered his knowledge of the afterlife from whatever source he could access.

There is so much evidence to prove that we all survive death but sadly so few people bother to pursue this knowledge during life. Most people start to take an interest when they are confronted with the great pain of losing a loved one.

Don would often say, "I wonder what it is really like on the other side?" Well, within two weeks of his passing, he was communicating in writing through his youngest daughter Nicola and telling her exactly what it was like.

Nicola had not been a medium prior to her Father's passing and had no deep knowledge of spiritualism or the afterlife; neither had she read any books on the subject. She was a divorced lady with three young children under six to cope with. Hers was a practical world, which was soon to be turned upside down. Within six months, of Don's passing, in the August of 2001 she had become a deep trance medium.

When Nicola is in trance I am able to talk directly to Don and to many other's that come through to her - including the great physical medium Helen Duncan to whom Nicola bears a striking resemblance. Many of Don's communications are in the main body of this book.

It is such a thrill to talk to him again. It's just like having the same telephone conversations with him that we had when we were together on the earth plane. Indeed it is just as if he'd never gone. I would often say to my friends 'I'm going to talk to Don tonight would you like to ask him anything?'

As I stated earlier there are no coincidences and I am certain that Don is playing a big part in the shaping of my future life, as in what happened about 18 months ago.

I was watching a video 'The Science of Eternity' which had been written and presented by Alan Pemberton. Basically it involved a series of interviews with people, including the renowned David Icke and several scientists investigating the scientific evidence proving life after death. I had a strong feeling that I should meet Alan, so I sent a letter with a photo of Don enclosed, to one of the scientists who kindly forwarded it to Alan. Imagine my surprise when I got a phone call from Alan saying, 'I am looking at this photograph of your dead husband and he is totally insistent that I call you. I don't normally do this but he is so persistent. He just won't leave me alone! Perhaps we should meet and look at those letters which are coming from Spirit?'

We did meet and I am happy to say still remain very good friends. I am a medium and he, a poet, writer and broadcaster. As time passed, it became very apparent that Don has a strong and affectionate connection with Alan, although they had never met on the earth plane. He had obviously selected Alan to help write the book, knowing that he was a writer with a solid understanding of spiritual matters.

I hope you enjoy the following selection of letters from Don's new world of spirit. I also hope they give you; the reader, the assurance that there is no death, and along with Alan's comfort poems bring further affirmation of the next world to which we shall all travel one day.

Rosemary Spencer, September 2003

Many Think It's Wrong

Many think it's wrong it seems
To speak at all of death
Birth is looked on joyously
Both are marked by breath
The first gasp of the infant
The last breath of the dying
Both of them are nothing more
Than nature loves sighing
To each a start
To each an end
So let there be no tears
The chains of life
Are freed by death
Along with doubts and fears
So we who have life
Can touch with love
The lives of those we meet
Leaving the souls who've travelled on
To sit at the master's feet
For who are we to speculate
That death will not transcend
The fear we have of nothingness
That death must be the end
So do not think of darkness
When you grieve for those who've gone
They're just a little step ahead
The road we'll travel on

Alan Pemberton

Don's Passing

Don was a builder, who took great pride in his work. He was also a proud and very handsome man, who women found irresistible. A real charmer with a great sense of fun – a lovely man! Then, in his sixties, after a lifetime of good health he began to experience problems.

His pride was dealt a dreadful blow when he had a stroke and had to walk with a stick. The stroke put paid to any physical work so his life was transformed over night. Surely of all the gifts that life can bring, good health is the greatest of them all?

Previous to this Don had suffered a dreadful attack of shingles - a horrible, painful, ugly condition which takes a great deal of time to heal. This was followed by high blood pressure, and sugar diabetes, which caused a lot of other painful ailments to develop. He was in constant pain and hated walking around with a stick. He was often hospitalised for long periods of time.

We lived in Weymouth at the time and this is where he died. As we shall learn from the letters, he passed very quickly and was shocked and confused when he was out of his physical body watching me desperately trying to revive him on the bed. I couldn't of course. Don was dead - at least I thought he was!

My heart goes out to anyone who has suffered bereavement. It really is the worst of all earthly pains. It eats at the very soul and for a while makes normal life a living nightmare. Even with my solid belief in an afterlife, I was completely brokenhearted by his passing and so desperately wanted him back. He didn't let me down on that front, as we shall see.

During the early stages of my bereavement, I felt very alone and was already planning to move from Weymouth back to Bournemouth. Within two weeks of Don's passing, I had a visit from my stepdaughter Nicola and my three lovely step-grandchildren. One evening during their stay, Nicola was missing for some time and I became curious, wondering what she was doing. I found her in a bedroom, sitting on the bed, scribbling madly on a writing pad. "What are you doing dear?" I asked.

She told me she had just seen, written on the wall above the bed on which Don had died, the words, 'GOD BLESS'. She had tried to rub the words off but to no effect. Then, suddenly, the words simply faded from view. I then asked her what she was writing?

"I'm getting messages from Dad! He's telling me what's happened to him since his passing."

This was the beginning of a flood of communication, which came initially through Nicola's pen. Later she was to fall into deep trance and bring many people through from spirit. These included not only Don but her spirit guide 'Rainbow Cloud', but more of this later.

I have already stated that Nicola had no knowledge of the spirit world prior to her experience and had certainly not been aware that she had a spirit guide, which of course we all have!

My first awareness of her deep trance mediumship occurred when I visited her at her home. She was sitting in a chair when suddenly she closed her eyes and started making strange movements with her hands. It looked as if she was either gathering energy from the room or connecting with invisible forces. She was then in trance. This pattern persists whenever she enters her trance state. Nicola tells me, that from her perspective, it starts with a slight headache and then an intense feeling of cold.

She appears to enter an area of blue light where she is suspended for the duration of the trance. She is then taken over by various spirit entities that wish to pass on messages and information, one of which I referred to earlier, the famous medium Helen Duncan, who is a frequent visitor and to whom Nicola bears a remarkable resemblance.

The normal sequence of events, once in trance, is for a deep masculine voice to come through her lips saying, "I am Rainbow Cloud, Nicola's guide. I am going to bring Don through to you."

The first time I got a message in this way, Don's voice said to me 'Hi Babe, I'm so happy to be able to talk to you'. This was amazing because he always called me Babe in life.

He spoke of his concern about my notion to move. He advised me that a move to Bournemouth was a good idea and that I would find a nice flat and eventually be happy. He told me that I would not be able to view the property that I had planned to visit on that day because the agent couldn't get the keys. He said that, instead, the agent would call me the next day. Well, of course, that's exactly what happened.

There was no doubt in my mind that this was my Don, because of the manner in which he instructed me on my affairs, something which he always did on the earth plane with the same characteristic bluntness.

Although later on in this book, Don describes his own arrival in spirit, it is worth noting that many entities that have communicated from Spirit, through various mediums, speak about hospitals where people go on arrival, particularly those who have endured long periods of ill health. It seems that we arrive in spirit in precisely the same state of mind that we had when on earth. So many frail souls believe they are still suffering from earthly illnesses.

It takes time to adjust to a mental rather than a physical dimension. The hospitals in spirit are designed to help people make this vital adjustment and to heal lingering phantom pains and ailments. Rather like the person who has had a limb amputated but still feels sensations where the limb use to be.

These hospitals are apparently set in beautiful grounds and are an oasis of peace and tranquillity. A place where kind spirits patiently free newcomers from their pains and explain how they need suffer no more. They are also gently guided into their new life in the world of spirit. So many people that pass over remain unaware that they have died. In some cases it takes very long periods of time to bring these spirits to the realisation that they have left the earth plane.

It appears that there are various regions or realms in the world of spirit. There are the highest realms where the most highly evolved spirits dwell, just as there are the lowest regions where the gross spirits find themselves. These may include, gross un-evolved spirits that dwell in darkness and have to be guided out of their ignorance by visits from evolved beings that instruct them on the nature of their dying and how they may progress to other levels.

We are all obliged to review our earth life - good and bad. This information is held in something called the Akashic record. How many times have we heard people, who have been close to death, say 'I saw the whole of my life flash before me'. Nothing is lost!

For the sake of simplicity we may describe the place that most people travel to after death as the 'Summerlands' others may prefer to think of this place as Heaven. This is where relatives and loved ones are waiting to welcome us into the world of spirit and where Don's hospitals are situated.

It would appear from Don's writings and from many other sources, that in spirit we are attracted to certain people that have a similar vibration to ourselves. Just as in life, we are attracted to certain people and sometimes repelled or indifferent to others. Don talks about soul groups and refers to the group he belongs to being 'one unit of light'. The group appears to reflect and share, similar spiritual levels - levels to which they had aspired whilst on earth. We may for instance think that we shall remain, in spirit, with the friends, relatives and loved ones that we knew on earth. This may not be the case, since they may now belong to a different soul group or vibration. Though, according to Don, we may, if we wish, visit those in other realms. I am sure it will all make sense once we enter spirit.

We need to make a leap of faith to begin to believe in the afterlife, largely because we are asked to believe that which we can rarely see or experience. Science in the form of Quantum Physics, however, informs us that just because we cannot see something it does not mean it doesn't exist. We are actually formed by invisible building blocks of energy in motion.

The bugs, which give us diseases, are invisible to the naked eye and we cannot see the atoms, which form the building blocks of our material world. Invisible atoms vibrating at different frequencies form the whole of life. We are surrounded by a whole world of invisible structures, without which physical life would not exist.

We cannot see television and radio waves. Millions of messages travel electronically over this planet every second of the day and night. We receive them but we cannot see them.

Everything is energy in one form or another. We are all part physical, part spiritual. That part of us which survives death is of a different vibration than that of the physical. It is the same vibration as the world of spirit. I am convinced that an explanation of the world of spirit will one day be proved closer to Physics than to the supernatural. One great master, said, 'In my Fathers' house are many mansions'.

Worlds within worlds, also has rather an interesting ring about it.

Don's letters begin

After Don had made the initial contact, when Nicola was in my house in Weymouth, Nicola returned to her house in Bournemouth and was very soon on the phone to me saying that she was being bombarded with messages from her dad. I was of course overjoyed and anxious to read the letters. Within a couple of days I travelled to Bournemouth myself and stayed with Nicola. I had already decided to live there, since I had many friends in the town and loved the Bath Road Spiritualist Church, where as a medium, I was often on platform (a public performance of clairvoyance).

Imagine my joy when I read those letters. I now knew that my husband was still alive and able to make contact. The following letters are just a few of the stream of communication that initially came through, ten days after Don's passing on the 14th of August 2001. Although later on, I received a few letters myself the bulk of the messages came through Nicola and are still arriving to this day.

Don was a dedicated father and grandfather. He was always anxious that his three daughters and numerous grandchildren were well and their affairs in order. He was a bit of a worrier but then being born under the sign of Virgo, this was to be expected. In my experience a Virgo without a worry, is like a fish out of water - to worry is part of the Virgo personality, just as homes are to Cancerian people, like myself.

Don's First Letter

Let me explain how I am on the other side of the rainbow. I am a proud man and had never been ill, until during the last couple of years my body slowly deteriorated and ceased to function, as it should. My sugar diabetes took over and my sugar levels became very high which in the end, caused my passing.

I experienced no fear as I stepped into the next world but I was disturbed on seeing old familiar faces. They were the faces of friends and relatives, who I had known on earth and who I knew had passed on years before. Then I saw my physical body lying on the bed. I was totally shocked and gazed in disbelief, but I was comforted by the spirit people around me. I saw my dear wife trying desperately to revive me. I tried to reassure her that it was no use trying to save me but she fought hard and tears of sadness flowed from within my spiritual being.

My Father-in Law, who was beside me, took my hand and said, "Come on Son, let's go home." At that moment it had not really registered with me that I was in spirit form since when I looked into the bedroom mirror, I appeared to be alive.

It was difficult to come to terms with the fact that I had completed my life on earth and that the time had come to move on and continue my work in spirit.

My Father-in-law then made me laugh when he said to me, "Do you want to walk or fly, you can do either here?" This confused me a bit but we finally decided to fly.

We entered a tunnel full of radiant colour upon colour and throughout this colour shone a brilliant light. The beauty of flashing lights, as we travelled through the tunnel, overwhelmed me. At the end of the tunnel we entered into a clear blue light, where the rest of my family were waiting.

I had heard that stillborn children return to spirit and continue to grow and mature. So my proudest moment came when I was united with my handsome son, Mathew, who had been stillborn, so had never touched the earthplane. What a joy it was to see him grown up and looking strong and well. My dogs, Tammy and Lady were so excited. I also met my two beautiful granddaughters (who had also been stillborn) their hair was soft and curly and their eyes twinkled like stars. I did, however, still feel tears of pain for those who I had left behind but I was also moved by the wondrous beauty of this vibrant place. I was determined to make contact as quickly as I could with those loved ones I had left behind and just say 'Don't worry, I'm fine'

I realised that the only person I could do this through was my youngest daughter, Nicola, as her link with me is so strong. She also has a very clear channel and an aura of radiant colours. I knew that through Nicola, I could contact my loving wife and tell her what it was really like here.

I had been convinced of an afterlife for sometime preceding my death and had tried to convince many people that I had met during my life, not to fear death. I was now more determined than ever to get the message across of what life was like on this side and that life goes on. So I ask people to please not judge too harshly those people who do not believe, even if at times you have doubts yourself.

I am learning all the time and there really is such a lot to learn. It's rather like being a child again experiencing life for the first time. Let's face it I have an eternity to adjust!

I am sad for those who I have left behind but so happy that I have forged this link with Nicola. She will have this gift for the rest of her life. I would say to everyone,

never fear death for there is nothing to fear. In the world of spirit there is only peace and love.

Don

Don reflects on the hospital grounds in spirit

It's so lovely here, sunlight all the time. The atmosphere is so tranquil and within these hospital grounds soft - healing music fills the air.

I have a guide who calls himself 'Two feathers' he is with me all the time. I had been contacted by him whilst on earth, when I sat in a circle. He is always advising me on different issues of life. I do still grieve, you know, but I can't be held back. I have to move on. I am slowly coming to terms with my passing and look forward to telling you what it is like on this side.

I love these hospital grounds, so full of vibrant colours and surrounded all the time by this heavenly music. I am learning to travel by thought. This takes some practise but I'll get it right in time. I just feel at such peace. People come and go as they do on earth. The feeling is that we are all part of one team.

The sea here is crystal clear and you can see your face in it. Children play at the seaside as they do on earth. There are always helpers around them.

Trees seem to pulsate with energy and their leaves are full of light but with a different texture than on earth. No words can really describe the beauty of this spiritual place.

Don

To Nicola when she was feeling a bit low

Call me by my name and I'll be there when you are in need. I will comfort you, since I know how much you miss me. Remember I am not gone, I am alive and well and living on. Please try not to be sad. Think on me as a free person who is still able to fill your heart with joy, just as I tried to do on earth.

You will be amazed at my stories and accounts, now that I'm on the other side.

I will try and convey the true meaning of spiritual life so that you may share this with others who are missing their loved ones or who have a fear of death. I will only give you truth about what goes on in this beautiful place.

Love
Dad

Heaven's Side

When the storm inside is raging
When the night has trapped your fears
When the nightmare starts unfolding
When you cannot stem your tears
I shall see you in your sorrow
I shall feel your deep despair
Softly fold my arms around you
Let you know that I am there
I have passed the veil of knowledge
Leaving you with earthly gloom
Heaven floats and flows between us
Death is neither end nor doom
In the sunshine of our memories
Spun by silver thread so fine
Lives a picture of our loving
All is saved which is divine
Hold our love which is forever
Call me and I'm by your side
Trust the voice you hear within you
Sending love from heaven's side

Alan Pemberton

Don is still in spirit hospital

Life is a dream and I am learning new things everyday. I know you are all still grieving but time will heal and your pains will lessen.

I love Rosemary and you very much and will always be around when you need me.

Sometimes I feel a bit lonely as I sit in my hospital bed. The strange thing is that I feel so at peace. This makes the feeling of loneliness rather beautiful in a way that is hard to describe. It's all part of the healing process, I suppose.

I am not far away - not as far as you think and don't worry because we will all meet again. Darling Rosemary, you will always be so special to me and I take pride in the wonderful things you do for others. The day will come when you will find new love. You are very strong in spirit and have a lot of living to do. Just remember that I shall always love you - be happy!

Don

Reflecting on why he had to go to spirit so early

I wonder, at times when I am lost in thoughts, why God took me to this Kingdom of love so early? I know in a way that it was the right thing at the right time because my body was slowly giving in. I did realise at this time though, that although my body was growing weaker, my soul awareness was becoming stronger. In a way I was being prepared for the journey to spirit.

It really is a lovely thing to know that I am still loved and highly thought of on earth - a good feeling!

I know that I shall continue my work from the world of spirit. I want to bring comfort to those people on earth who are suffering from loneliness. I want to try and bring joy to those whose hearts are bleak and unhappy, to bring hope to their souls.

My prayers, of course, are also for my own family and friends. I miss them all but their earthly life must run its course. The worst thing is to know that they are grieving for me. I have fulfilled my earthly duties and it is now up to them to put the pieces of their own jigsaw together. Of course I hate to see them in confusion, but I am comforted by the knowledge that everything will pass, and I now know what is waiting to greet them when on their passing.

Don

Dimensions of the Spirit world

I am somewhere over the rainbow, in a land of brilliant light, our spirit here seems to light up with rays of exquisite colours. It is a rich magical land, a part of Gods Kingdom, just as the earth is. I feel as if I am part of one unit of light and energy, completely surrounded by these beautiful colours.

Many souls can visit the earth and bring healing to those in need. I am told that I shall be one of those lucky ones. Angels respond to earthly prayers. Believe in the power of angels. Sometimes they manifest as ordinary people. I can understand you being sceptical about this but it is possible that people talk to angels and never realise it.

Earthly life is a bit like a roller-coaster ride. I understand now that everyone is born and live their earthly life for a reason. Life, it seems, is for learning lessons, building the spirit and thus perfecting their immortal souls. Sometimes many lives are needed to accomplish this.

Those souls, who are incapable of recognising their mistakes, are known in spirit as lost souls. On entering spirit they inhabit the lower realms, which are darker than those of the Summerlands. Higher souls visit these people and try and help them to understand their mistakes. They are persuaded that to advance from these realms they must become less selfish and not think only of themselves. Only by helping others can they achieve this shift. They are given the opportunity to do this, through the will of the visiting angelic forces.

Don

A Love letter from Don to Rosemary

No words can describe my love for you or express how I feel for you. You gave me tender loving care throughout my illness. You acted like an angel that gave me hope, faith, and encouraged me to do things on my own. You were not ready to give up on me and were determined that we would fight the illness and pull through together. I can't thank you enough for all you tried to do for me.

We often used to talk and imagine what life would be like on the other side of the rainbow and how wonderful it would be. Well, now I am here and I can tell you that everything we imagined is true but more wonderful than we could have ever imagined.

The colours are so beautiful, a world of splendid and varied rays of light. Everything is light in form and soft textures.

My Pearl, I am very much myself and am fully aware that I am on the other side. I am as fit as a fiddle and just as handsome as ever but so much lighter in form. I am at peace and often with members of my family who passed on before me.

Physically I feel wonderful - free of pain and much younger in mind and body.

When on earth we have guides who try to influence our lives but here we meet them face-to-face. They still continue to teach their wisdom and offer rare love indeed.

I am always by your side
Don

Don remembers seeing himself in his coffin

Now that my family knows that I am living on, it is great to see them coming to terms with my death without too much ongoing grief. If only people would realise that we all pass to the next world, good, bad and ugly, the pains of bereavement would be more tolerable. We live on. We don't just disappear. Life is formed by energy and energy cannot be destroyed. The physical body dies but the etheric body moves on.

It was my time to move on from the earth plane and to leave my friends and family in order to join this wonderful world of spirit.

I was really scared at first, when I saw my family and friends who had already passed. You can imagine the joy I experienced on meeting my son Mathew (Mathew was miscarried at six months) I cried like a baby and felt so proud of him.

Another early shock was seeing my body lying in the coffin. I knew that body lying there had been full of pain and simply couldn't take anymore of it. I had so many things wrong with me; there was no relief. Being here has set me free from all pain and I feel young at heart again.

Don

Another message for Rosemary
about the spirit world

It is hard I know for everyone when we lose a loved one but life does and must go on.

Just know that my love for you pours out and is always there for you to feel. This heaven is such a beautiful place, so tranquil and so, so relaxing. Let no one tell you there is no life on the other side - there is and it is literally sheer heaven!

Once you are here your whole outlook changes. It's like reading a history book of your own life and realising and learning from your mistakes. Imagine a series of doors, as one closes another opens and this keeps happening until you have accepted and learned from your mistakes. When you have finally learned your lessons from life, the final door opens into a world of beautiful light - a light of many colours, which are rich and vibrant. It is really a whole new world. Non-believers find this hard to imagine but it is very real indeed.

I feel as if I have gone back to the beginning again, like a child starting all over again. I can hop, skip and jump as I like. All my limbs feel free and I am able to roam where I wish, free of the pains which crippled me on earth. My energy levels are amazing. I am aware that I am living in a spiritual form in my new kingdom.

Dearest Pearl, please tell them at the spiritual church, what I am telling you about this magical world. Non-believers must be told about the love and the great peace they will find. We all belong to one Great Spirit.

As one enters the spirit world all suffering stops and to be living in a new world is quite amazing. Maybe it's selfish because we leave our loved ones behind but to be free of pain is so incredible.

What is death? It is just a word. You have nothing to fear when you pass, just a sense of utter relief. One enters the world of spirit so quickly and peacefully. You do not carry the pain; it releases itself and dies with the physical body.

Love always
Don

Don tries hard to describe the wonders of the spirit world

Everything here is like a field of energy. I walk around in what seems like an aura of multi-coloured lights that bounce in all directions. In the spirit world the trees seem to give out healing rays and energy flows from the plants and flowers. It is hard to describe everything in words because, in a sense, there are no words to explain what it is really like. It is as if the very landscape is full of the music of energy. The grass shimmers sending out delightful rays of colour.

Spirits greet one another by mind and thought but we can talk if we want to, just as we did on earth. We seem to feel wiser or to carry more knowledge here than we had when we passed. This does not mean that we stop learning - far from it.

Don

More about the composition
of the spirit world

We live in this world of light and brilliant colours. We emanate the colours of our individual souls. I can only describe it as a world of light and energy. The spirit world has form but it is of a much lighter quality than the physical world.

Our guides and helpers, urge us to learn, understand and move closer to our higher selves, to which we are all connected. Perfection seems to be a complete state of harmony within our higher self or soul.

Light seems to be the fuel, which energises our spirit souls. We are recharged by this all-pervading energy source. Although we are still the same person as we were on earth, we are much lighter in form - free as a butterfly. We can still feel every limb and seem to have a greater understanding and a clearer mind.

There is a common desire amongst us that we need to carry the message to those on earth that life continues after death. So many people are sceptical but we can understand why they find it so hard to believe.

Initially our thoughts revolve around the loved ones we have left behind but as I have said so many times, life must go on. We learn from the mistakes we made in the physical world and we reflect on these mistakes, often becoming very distressed when reviewing some of the things we deeply regret having done. It's not pleasant coming to terms with life's errors but one realises how valuable the experience of earthly life really is. Our earth history is so precious. It is so hard getting things right if we haven't experienced what it feels like to get it wrong. Pain so often leads to wisdom.

We learn how important it is for people to listen to the quiet voice, which is the voice of our spirit clothed in a body of flesh, just like an overcoat.

Life really is what we make it. The inner self is far more important than the outer body. The spirit travels on and the physical body decays.

Don

To Nicola Sept 1991

Call me by my name and I'll be there when you need me. I am still able to hold your hand and comfort you, as I am not gone. I am alive and well and living on. Do not feel sad, as I am free of pain.

I will fill your heart with joy and you will be amazed at my stories, now that I am on the other side. You will learn and know the true meaning of spiritual life and what it is like to live in the next world.

Dad

In Peace Go Home

Through veils of mist may you ascend
To promised planes of love
Where comfort shall await you
In those Summerlands of love
Although my grief is deep and raw
Although my pain is great
I know that you are still with me
I know that you will wait
For in God's time we'll meet again
Of this I am quite sure
I loved you so much on this earth
In absence even more

Alan Pemberton

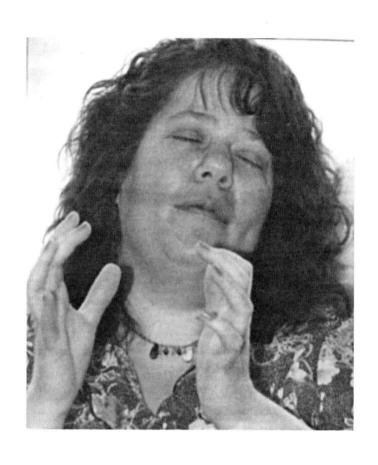

Picture of Nicola in a Trance
(By courtesy of Bournemouth Echo)

Rosemary and Nicola
(By courtesy of Bournemouth Echo)

The Bath Road Spiritualist Church

Don and Rosemary on their wedding day at

Bath Road Spiritualist Church

Psychic drawings through Rosemary Spencer from the Spirit World

Strange things happen around Rosemary and Nicola

Apart from the letters from spirit, Don is very active around mine and Nicola's houses, amongst other things objects move and fly mysteriously through the air.

Four years before he died, Don had purchased a Helium Rabbit on a stick for his granddaughter, Janine. The rabbit was stuck in a vase and at the time of writing is still there. The remarkable thing is that six years on, the rabbit remains inflated. This is despite the fact that the rabbit's head once fell off the stick and bounced across the room and onto the bed where Nicola was resting. She stuck it back on with cellotape and the rabbit remained inflated. I myself have witnessed the rabbit twirling around in the vase. The rabbit's ears change position, sometimes drooping and sometimes sticking up or pointing forward.

Don will bang doors, open bins, open car doors and move objects. He once threw a vase of flowers from the top of my TV three times in a row until I realised that he was trying to draw my attention to a saucepan that I had forgotten was on the cooker. I had left it boiling for over two hours. When I eventually went into the kitchen, I picked up the saucepan with a tea cloth but found the pan to be stone cold yet the ring was still glowing hot.

Jars of baby food have been suspended in the air with a

spoon, twirling above the jar on its own. Another time I had returned from a journey to find that my kettle had been switched on, ready for me to make a cup of tea on arrival. All hard to believe I know, but non-the-less true experiences.

Two weeks before Don passed he kept appearing at the bottom of Nicola's bed with an Egyptian dressed in gold. This same character is mentioned later in Don's letters from spirit. When Nicola told her Father that he was appearing with the Egyptian, he did not understand what she was talking about.

Don often visits his Granddaughter, Janine. She refers to him as 'Papa' Don. Janine was always very close to her Grandfather. She says that he often visits her in the night and they play together. She tells her mother that he brings a dog with him. It is her grandmother's dog, the same dog that suddenly appeared on a painting of Don's dead wife Jean.

Once during a family trip in my car to visit friends I was told off by Janine for locking Papa Don in the car when we got out. Often Janine will say Papa Don is outside a window waving. Janine also has a habit of blaming her Grandfather for a lot of strange happenings saying, 'Papa Don did it, or Papa Don told me to.'

Janine also informed her Mother that Papa Don had once killed a lot of pigeons. Her mother remembered that twenty years ago; long before Janine was born; her Father had indeed done just that. A friend had had a problem with some pigeons in their loft and Don had helped out by shooting them. An act that he probably deeply regrets in spirit.

Nicola's Father isn't the only person that comes through Nicola when in deep trance. She has often been taken over by the great medium, Helen Duncan. Before Nicola brings other spirits through, her main guide 'Rainbow Cloud' introduces them by name. Nicola's voice changes with each new visitor. She can remain in trance for up to two hours at a time and has no recollection of what has been said when she comes out of trance.

I have been privileged to be present on all occasions, since Nicola only ever goes into trance when I am present. I act as her gatekeeper between this world and the next. A few others have seen and heard Nicola in trance and have been able to hold conversations with the spirit visitors. These visitors include children who come through with little messages. For a variety of good reasons it would not be wise to mention the names of those who have come through, since it maybe upsetting for the relatives and in some cases very dangerous for Nicola.

When Nicola comes out of a trance she has great difficulty focusing her eyes and feels very low in energy.

She recently had her knowledge of the spirit world boosted following an out-of-body experience.

People who have been proclaimed clinically dead but are later revived usually record such experiences. Most give an all too similar account of travelling through a long dark tunnel into a bright world of light where their dead relatives are waiting to greet them. They are often advised to turn back because it is not their time to pass. People that have experienced this (and there are hundreds of recorded cases - many from baffled surgeons and doctors) speak of an overwhelming feeling of peace and contentment, which they never forget. It is a life changing experience since these people no longer have any fear of death, indeed they cannot wait to have that sublime feeling again.

Nicola's out of body experience

Nicola had been relaxing in a chair when she suddenly seemed to shoot out of her body. The following account is what she experienced.

I came across a door that was battered and worn and I was very curious to know what was beyond this door, which was aged with time. I nervously opened the door and to my amazement, saw a beam of light. Slowly I walked into the light and the door closed behind me. At first I found it difficult to focus, since the beam of light shone so brightly. I started to walk cautiously through the beam. Then, after a while, the beam of light faded away. I turned around and there stood an old man dressed in a gown. He wore a cross around his neck and carried a pole, which appeared to be wrapped in gold and had sparkling gems on the top. He waved his hand and said, "Come child, come." I slowly walked towards him and he took my hand and whispered, "Close your eyes my child, I want to take you somewhere special." I clung onto the old man's hand nervously. After a few minutes he said, "You can open your eyes now."

I opened my eyes and was astonished to find myself standing in a beautiful garden, which shone with bright unearthly colours. I saw in the distance a wooden seat and there was somebody sitting there. I was curious about this person so I moved towards the seat. It was a man seated with his back to me. I felt the urge to put my hands on his shoulders. He suddenly turned and to my astonishment saw it was my dad.

"But Dad, you went to spirit ages ago, how come you are here and alive?" Tears started to stream down my face and feeling his muscles I said, "But you are so real and alive."

He rested his hands on mine and replied, "Child, we brought you here to see for yourself what the spirit world is like. You are having an out-of-body experience."

I then said "Oh Dad, I miss you so much but you have changed a lot since I last saw you, you are so young and your skin feels like silk and your complexion so fresh."

Then my mum appeared along with my granddad, my brother and my nan (who was Don's mother). My mum looked beautiful - a typical English rose. My brother was very handsome - so much like Dad.

My mother was holding a baby in her arms. "This is your baby, she said, the one you thought you had lost. As you can see she is very much alive and so like you. She's got your nose. Would you like to hold her?"

I took the baby in my arms. The baby smiled and made gurgling sounds. I kissed her and as I handed her back to Mum I said, "God bless, my darling."

Dad then took hold of me and we walked arm in arm in the beautiful garden. The air was full of the scented fragrance of flowers. Dad said, "Put your ear to the flowers and you will hear soft melodies." He was right. I felt so proud walking with my Dad again.

Dad then turned and smiled at me, saying, "Before I go…"

"Oh, don't go Dad," I pleaded.

He continued, "Yes dear, I must, but I want you to have this book. It is your book of life and very special. It will show you your true way."

"Can you explain in more detail?" I said.

He replied, "Since coming to spirit, I have been watching over you. I have seen a different light in you. You have crossed many bridges and have come a long way, since my passing. You have gained strength from God allowing you to move forward in life and look after your children. At times you have weakened but you climbed back up the ladder and went on. This book will help you on your pathway. It is to encourage you to do more things in your life, to test your strengths and weaknesses. Believe in your work and choose words carefully and wisely. Make more of your gift. Since I am in spirit I cannot be there for you as I have my duties to attend to here, and most of these involve helping others who are in difficulties.

"You have to finally decide what to do in your life. We can guide you and help as much as we can but in the end it is up to you. You have gained much knowledge and have grown up a lot since I left. I have seen you perform with your mediumistic gifts, but remember it must not take up the whole of your life. Make the most of your life on the earth plane. I have to go now, so God bless you."

He faded into the background and the old man re-appeared. He took my hand again and asked me to close my eyes. Suddenly I was back in the beam of light and then the old battered door was once again before me. I went through the door and it closed behind me. I continued walking. I felt so much warmth and goodness around me. It felt as if I had been given new energies and a new lease of life. It was a wonderful experience. It will stay with me for the rest of my life!

I'd rather see you smiling

You must not think that I have gone
Please don't grieve or pine
I'd rather see you smiling
Laughing-working-looking fine
Death is an exciting key
Which opens many doors
It leads us into other worlds
Quite similar to yours
Life is not an accident
Death is not the end
God designed a mystery
Life and death do blend
So do not think that I have gone
Please don't brood or pine
I'd rather see you smiling
Laughing – working- looking fine

Alan Pemberton

The Tube, Helix or Tunnel

Perhaps it is worthwhile spending a little time and a few words here in an attempt to explain how spirit entities claim they visit the earthplane.

We know from the accounts of those who went through a near-death-experience that they all felt they had travelled through a tunnel or passage. They felt no fear; on the contrary; they all claim it was a sublime feeling of peace and tranquillity as they passed upward and into the light at the other end. This indicates that there is something, which connects this world with other worlds.

Many esoteric writers and thinkers have tried to explain this as something akin to the Double Helix, which is found in the structure of DNA molecules. The information coming from spiritual entities that use this structure to visit the earthplane say it is like a coil of brilliant energy through which they pass back and forth. In one of Don's letters he tries to explain the feelings associated with this journey.

This brings us back to the problem; a subject we briefly touched on earlier in this book, the difficulty most of us have when asked to believe in the structural nature of things existing in worlds of invisibility.

What is certain is that we are all built upon these invisible structures. The whole of our material world, including us, the universe and beyond is composed of atoms in movement. Nothing is really solid. It all depends on the speed at which these atoms vibrate as to whether we can see an object or not. Just because we cannot see something, does not mean that it doesn't exist. We perceive and experience our material world through our senses, which are adjusted to work within a specific vibration. Reality as we know it is nothing more than energy in movement working under a Divine Will which we will probably never understand. It is this divine intelligence that is able to create multiple forms by manipulating varying rates of vibration. The next letter from Don allows us to see this from his perspective.

Alan Pemberton

Hoops of rich vibrant colour

We come down to earth through a tube of light, which shimmers, with such an aura of colour this is an electrifying experience, which fills us with energy.

Inside the tube are rays or hoops of rich vibrant colours. We pass through these hoops with such incredible speed when entering the earth world and returning to spirit.

Light is our source of energy and this wonderful light surrounds us in spirit. It is this light which constantly re-energises our spirit bodies. We think upon this brilliant light as God.

Don

Don visits the children's Realms

I feel the need to communicate with you today, as I feel so relaxed and full of energy. In fact I feel so good I want to shout about it. I am a free spirit free from pain.

Today my son Mathew is visiting me and so is my guide 'Two feathers' along with another guide who is an Egyptian. I get the feeling he is more of a helper.

Mathew, my son, who never touched the earth plane, is such a lovely lad. Happiness surrounds him and he is always joyfully explaining the wonders of life in the spirit world. He says we continue to carry on with our duties just as we did on earth. The difference is in the quality of life; it is so different here, it is difficult for you to believe, I know, but one touch on any object and light shines out in all directions. It could be a door or book - everything glows with different colours!

We can build our own homes with pure thought - it's amazing.

We have a different kind of love here for each other. It's a spiritual love. Always remember you have eternity to look forward to.

Today we are all going to visit the Children's Realms to see my Grandchildren, Karen and Renee. It's a very special place and the children have special helpers. They also have toys and dolls just as they do on earth. Babies have their own environment and are cared for by their own helpers. There is so much love poured out in these Realms.

My son Mathew tells me he spent a long time in these places but has, of course, now grown up and progressed.

They are young souls who are taught about the history of life. They learn so much before re-entering the earthplane. So much time is given to the babies. They are of all colours and creeds. I can tell you it doesn't matter if you are rich or poor when you enter the spirit world. We enter the earthplane with nothing and we return with nothing.

Don

Follow Your Dreams

Follow your dreams
Whatever they are
Let no one turn your head
It's a very short time we are living
Too short to be hampered by dread
Don't listen to those who will tell you
That your dreams are impractically spun
You can't live the life of another
You'll never get anything done
So cherish your goals and ambitions
They're given to you to fulfil
A voice deep within can be trusted
To guide you and strengthen your will
There's nothing that you cannot conquer
There's nothing you cannot achieve
If your heart has a need
And your mind finds the seed
Harness hope and you're bound to succeed

Alan Pemberton

**Don came out of the spirit hospital
he built the house and garden of his dreams.**

My garden is filled with beautiful flowers. These flowers have a soft texture, rather like cotton wool. They also have wonderful colour, which are much lighter and more vibrant than flowers on the earth plane. If you put your ears to these lovely things you can hear the most beautifully melodic sounds. Every flower in my garden represents something to me and they never seem to die. The grass is so green and the trees so much brighter than those on earth. I am so proud of my heavenly garden.

I have a Robin, which visits me quite regularly. He sits on my bench and chirps away.

The garden has been created entirely from my own thoughts and is just how I wanted it to be. I remember that I was told this is what happened, when I was on the earth, at the time I found this hard to believe but it's true.

I spend a lot of time in the garden, reading books and thinking of my loved ones on earth. It's all so relaxing and the air is full of the wonderful scent of flowers. How lucky I am to have finally got the garden of my dreams - a haven of love and light.

Don

A letter to Rosemary

Feel my love around you all the time. Feel only happiness never be sad. I will be at your side when you need me. I want you and Nicola to settle down and get on with your lives. All the love in the world walks beside you both. Enjoy the beauties of the earth. Feel my presence around you. I am here right now, standing beside you and feeling radiant.

Life works in circles of light so enjoy the light of your sunshine and be happy. Enjoy the memories we shared and know that I shall always be on hand to guide you through your difficulties. God bless you.

Don

A reassuring letter to Nicola

God gave you this gift of mediumship. He wants you to tell the world that life does go on as normally in the spirit world as it does on earth. There really is no such thing as death - it only has meaning on earth. We just walk from our bodies into the next world and carry on living as normal. We can do so much over here but it's different and most things take practice. We also feel proud of our achievements here.

I am so happy to communicate with you and we will progress together as life goes on. So cheer up we will help and protect you at all times.

Love
Dad

The writer of this letter claimed she was Enid Blyton

My life is wonderful here as I lie back against a tree and admire the beautiful colours which surround me. Colours are constantly changing one to another. It is endlessly beautiful.

I love to draw animals - indeed it is my passion to draw animals! In the spirit world, animals are rather like humans in that they (you will find this hard to believe) can talk and communicate their thoughts. They have a very wide knowledge. The animals only show themselves when they want to.

As I sit under this tree, people also appear suddenly and then disappear. They may talk to me for a while and then vanish.

God has created this most amazing and beautiful place - pure magic, pure heaven.

As I sit drawing, a wild cat comes towards me, full of life and wanting fun. On earth he would never have approached me but they are very tame here and full of affection. He brushes his face against my gown, nudging me for attention.

"No" I say, "I am working. When I am finished I will give you a cuddle".

Like all cats he is determined to get his own way. So I give in and putting my pencil and paper down, he climbs on my lap. We play together for a while then together we set off to walk among the trees and flowers and heavenly scents.

It is his turn to be disturbed now, since a bee settles on the end of his nose. I laugh as he tries to gently shake it off. The bee flies off to the flowers and my friend scratches the end of his nose with his paw.

After a good run together through the fields, I fall down exhausted and he makes off on his own.

I now have to visit the Children's Realm, where I read and tell stories. This is a great treat for me, as I love their bright-excited eyes and their minds full of imagination

With love

Enid Blyton

Father Michael, who claims to have been a monk, when on earth, is identified in this letter.

I hope that I became a wise man when on earth. I always have believed in God and had a great faith. I am Father Michael and use to be a monk when on the earth plane. My work was to bring help, love and support to poor and unfortunate people.

In my time the poor people had to live by the seasons. Hard seasons often meant that crops were destroyed and the people went hungry. Lack of nourishment ensured that diseases of all sorts were prevalent. In those dark days we had nothing like the medicine you now have to help people recover.

I hope you don't mind me saying that I think people of your age take a great deal for granted. You have so much more than we had, education, medicine clothing, food, fuel and electricity. In my day we worked by candlelight.

Being a monk in my day was very harsh and we lived in silence. Work started in the early hours and finished well into the night. We suffered with sore hands and ugly, painful sores on our feet.

We were allowed very little food but I used to manage to stuff stale bread under my gown and give it to hungry children who ate it with such relish.

If I could find time, I would teach the children about life and read to them from the Bible. In those days the Bible was the only book we had to comfort us.

When I come to earth now and try to add light to their lives. I go to those who have nothing. I visit those who live on the streets and those who are suffering. I also try and comfort those who are ready to pass into this magical world of spirit.

I am pleased to be able to talk to you and tell you about this spirit realm. I am a spirit person now but I still come down to your world to ease suffering.

God Bless you
Father Michael

On assisting those who have just passed

When loved ones pass to spirit they first enter a place of peace where they are able to rest. Over a period of time we help them realise that they have died in an earthly sense. This can sometimes take quite a long time. Slowly we teach them to carry on life as normal and to do things just as they did on earth, believe me it is very similar here. They become part of our one big family. They have to learn that they form themselves and everything else by thought. Strange, I know, but most of them soon get the hang of it.

When we visit earth we are able to move small objects with thought. We are also able to give healing to those who are in need. We seem to have knowledge of what lies ahead for people. This all happens in spirit where life is so very precious.

Don

This lovely letter from Don arrived on Valentine day for Rosemary

My desire on Valentine day is to be with you in thought. I want to bring my rays of sunshine into your life and to thank you for being my precious wife.

I am always with you and I watch over you. I give you my healing hands and if you close your eyes and visualise me, I will come to you with open arms. My heart is always with you and this connection will never be broken.

There are times when I must step back but I am never far away - just a place somewhere over the rainbow where I watch the flowing water travel under the rainbow bridge. We will meet here one day and it will be so beautiful. I will be my usual chirpy self.

New love will come your way, you just need to be patient - just take your time and remember my love is always around you, it just pours from my heart.

You gave me strength and hope when I was weak. I pray each night for you and my family, just as I did when on earth. I still can't believe that I am here since I still feel so very much me. I do miss my little granddaughters and I often come to the earth plane and plant a kiss goodnight on their cheeks.

Your nature is as sweet as honey and whoever finds you will be a very lucky man, since your heart is always full of love.

So I end my Valentine message by saying, smile and I will smile with you. I am never far away. Give time to yourself and always go with the flow since every day of your life is a bonus.

Your loving husband, Don

Another letter purported to come from Enid Blyton

It is wise to fill yourself with as much of Mother Nature's beauty as you can. It is so important for the human soul yet, sadly, it seems to be ignored or taken for granted in your world of today.

I remember when I was a child how lovely it was to be free, smelling and running in the fresh air. I loved the flowers, especially the Bluebells and Buttercups blowing in a soft summer breeze. It was so exhilarating dashing through the wild grass and feeling so safe and happy.

There was of course no such thing as television in my day. I feel it is sad for the children to see so much violence and to have their innocence corrupted when they are so young. Television seems to rule their little lives. We made our own games and created make-believe worlds full of Cowboys and Indians, Pirates and Kings and Queens. We dressed up in fancy costumes and pretended to be whatever we wanted to be. We played catch, hide and seek and we shrieked with natural happiness.

The child's mind today is full of horrid images that are created by money seeking writers and producers. I find it very sad and believe that childhood should be spent in a lovely fantasy world of imagination.

I spent hours reading children's novels out in the fields or under trees. I loved to draw or just gaze at the beauty of nature. I was a child who looked at the world through innocent eyes. Even when I had grown up I remained innocent and childlike. I conveyed this in all my work and tried to ignore the evil destruction which man inflicted so cruelly on Mother Earth.

In nature we see the manifestation of the creators beautiful mind. During my earth life I was famous for my children's books.

God Bless You
Enid Blyton

Song of Life

The river flows and has no spite
Nor has the meadow flower
The breeze that dances through the corn
Is not in search of power
The birds which fill our life with song
Ask nothing in return his loving earth can only give
And from it we should learn
We treat our planet with contempt
Like ants we do devour
The body which supports all life
For wealth for self for power
We've lost our kinship with those friends
Who roam the earth and sea
They live their lives in fear of man
Who stole their harmony?
That we should look again and see
The bounties of this earth
Through eyes that see more truly
The love that gave it birth

Alan Pemberton

Perspective

A creator who gave us a planet as beautiful as the earth, a creator who gave us flowers, sunrise, blue oceans teaming with life, magnificent forests, sweet meadows, breathtaking wildlife, soft moss, frost, breeze, rain, springtime, smells, tastes, harvests, love, music, inspiring passion, creativity, compassion, friendships, autumn leaves and so much more, would never be as cruel as to present us with the ever-present agonies and pains of life without a loving agenda holding a deeper meaning. It simply does not add up - it makes no sense. Earth is our college, spiritual growth our subject, free will our test and eternal life, His promise.

Excerpt from 'Requiem' a book of poems and reflections by Alan Pemberton

When the doors of death are closed
The gates of heaven open
All is Well in Heaven

Taken from 'Requiem' by
Alan Pemberton

Nothing comes through Nicola without 'Rainbow Cloud's' presence. Rosemary, who has developed a gift for receiving images of people's guides. A selection of these extraordinary drawings are shown on pages. The word extraordinary is used because in real life, Rosemary is unable to draw even the simplest object. She is not an artist; these images are delivered from another place.

Why Should Death So Final Be?

Take comfort in the ancient lore
That death is nothing but a door
Through which we enter when first sent
Through which we pass when life is spent
Our journey be it long or short
Is clothed in flesh and held in thought
And briefly do we touch sweet time
With all its pains and loves sublime
On this great planet rolled in space
Adorned by God's creative grace
Which angels fashioned long before
Mankind walked on nature's floor
There is a fashion to deny
The spirit world to which we fly
If birth and life are mystery
Why should death so final be
Perhaps the purpose of our lives
Is hidden deep by wise disguise
So may the fruits of death be great
In world's we cannot contemplate
For what the human eye can't see
Should not be judged a fallacy
So little do we comprehend
How life and death may sweetly blend

Alan Pemberton

Conclusion

There are many more of Don's letters, which do not appear in this book. Some of them are deeply personal and best left unpublished. Hopefully my story has been both enlightening and entertaining. It is up to the reader to decide how much of this information they hold and what they wish to dismiss. All I can say is that this was our true experience and it brought such joy to our lives.

At times Don's communications are so effervescent and his description of the Spirit World so amazing that it is hard to believe. Yet, just imagine being in such a place and experiencing it for the first time, then his exhilaration becomes understandable.

My experience as a platform medium has proved to me conclusively that people do survive death and are anxious to communicate with us on earth. Sometimes when I am in the Spiritualist Churches and on platform, I have them queuing up to get a word in and what a joy it is when the person getting the message, recognises a description of their loved one who is eager to be heard.

I would say to anyone who is bereaved, get along to your local Spiritualist Church. Once you have received a message you will feel so much better and much more able to bear the pains of loss.

There are always questions that remain unanswered, and so many people are sceptical about other dimensions. I personally could never see the point in having a negative attitude to survival. It somehow diminishes the quality of life and makes suffering totally pointless.

I have also found that people who are total disbelievers tend to value material things over anything else and their lives seem to lack purpose. They are also often, discontented souls that can see no further than their next acquisition. As Don points out, you come in with nothing and you leave with nothing but your soul body.

People I meet either in the street or perhaps at church, ask me many questions about the Spirit World. I don't have all the answers but I would like to conclude this little book with a reflection, which I sometimes read before I start my platform work.

Who is God?

Has he form? Many people believe He is an energy of love and light expressing himself in many forms, but we are also told that we are made in his likeness.

I believe the likeness is a spiritual likeness, which should express itself with love and compassion towards all people and creatures. God obviously wears many overcoats and takes the form of whatever you want him to be.

When we were children we used to think of him as an elderly gentleman sitting on a throne, rather like Father Christmas. As Spiritualists we feel we have come to the knowledge that to have created the Universe and all the workings thereof, he cannot be described in earthly terms. His composition is beyond comprehension, rather like the ant that might gaze up at us in wonder.

God created us to be happy and to express himself through us. He gave us the reins and he gave us free will and because of this he does not interfere in our lives. He always supports us and gives us the opportunities to learn more about life and ourselves. I am not talking about the face we present to the world, but the true inner self - the spirit.

Often we close our minds to the simple truth and complicate our lives in pursuit of our physical desires. We create what happens to ourselves by thought and it is up to us to push out the dark negative thoughts and bring out the positive ones.

The dark thoughts; fear, anxiety, greed, jealousy, hatred, all go into the ether of life and link up with other peoples negative thoughts, creating a dark ugly matter which brings us all problems. Quiet thoughts and acts of a loving nature bring peace and happiness.

We are told that we are God's children but more than this we are part of him. We are a bit of the whole of creation - a segment of the orange and we therefore have great power within us, which many don't use. Should we not endeavour, to put things right in our families, relationships and on Mother earth?

I believe we have this special power to change things if we all pulled together. We should remember we are all part of the orange - we are not separate.

Jesus himself spoke of us being Gods. We can use the God power within; for good or for evil, it's our choice. Shall it be for mankind's betterment or for man's demise?

Memories of You

I had a drifting mood today
It stirred a thought or two
My mind went back to happy days
To memories of you
Our lives are like a tapestry
With two distinctive sides
The front a perfect picture
The back our secret hides
Our memories are built like this
Some are clear and real
Others travel in and out
With no specific feel
Life's phases too are tapestries
With textures of their own
Some we love and some we hate
From all of them we've grown
We gather wisdom from our pains
From torment we grow strong
Our spirit nurtured by mistakes
Still fated travels on
Perhaps one thing which stays the same
And will forever more
Is the love that we hold for another soul
The people we adore
So I had a drifting mood today
It stirred a thought or two
My mind went back to happy days
To memories of you.

Alan Pemberton

Part Two

Beyond the Rainbow

This communication arrived following the completion of the first part of the book.

It is a dramatic portrayal of the life and death of Lady Diana.

Diana speaks from the grave

I received a phone call from Rosemary Spencer, inviting me to go to the West Country to interview a very important person. As a freelance journalist I was naturally intrigued to know more.

I was told the person was Lady Diana and that she was desperate to talk and give her side of the many conflicting stories and theories about her death. I would be speaking to her through a deep trance medium.

In the past I have specialised in stories concerning Psychic Phenomena, for which I am quite well known in certain circles, so therefore I wasn't surprised that I had been contacted. This was not a subject I particularly wanted to get caught-up with but I agreed to go because I was very curious - who wouldn't be?

So I made the journey to an address near Bournemouth, which I had been given. After an edgy and exhausting journey, I found myself standing with Rosemary Spencer in a small flat illuminated largely by candlelight; I was introduced to the medium. She was a pleasant lady in her late thirties. After speaking to her for half an hour I realised that she was neither worldly nor particularly well read. Like many mediums I have met over the years, she was really rather a basic down to earth soul.

She told me that Lady Diana had been around her for days and was giving her a dreadful physical headache. She went on to say that Diana was anxious to put her side of the story and to talk to a member of the press. She was furious that people were still making money from her even though she was no longer alive, at least not in the physical world.

Later that evening we settled down and Rosemary said a few protective prayers and told me we would have to wait for the medium to go into trance. The first sign of this would be when she began to feel her body become icy cold. I watched as the medium's hand began making strange movement and very soon she was in trance.

A deep voice came from her throat. It was a male voice and was apparently her guide:

'Welcome, I am bringing somebody to talk to you.'
Was all he said.

Although the voice that came through was not like Diana's in anyway, it was full of emotion, urgency, outrage and extraordinary new details.

This is what she had to say:

Diana
'Thank you for coming. I am so angry at what's going on again and I want to put the record straight. Really, all I want is to be left in peace and to get on with my new life. Yes, it was a conspiracy - a real set-up. I can't prove it of course but I think the same as Dodi's Father does, that it was Prince Phillip who set me up. He never wanted me in the family. There is so much jealousy amongst the Royals. They hurt me so deeply and I really was the innocent victim.

At the time of the crash I was so happy with Dodi

and we were deeply in love. We were having such a lovely time at the Ritz Hotel. I had just told Dodi that I was ten weeks pregnant. He was thrilled but asked me whether I wanted to keep the baby. I said of course and he said then we would get married.

Question
How did you know you were pregnant?
Answer.
Harley Street specialist

Question.
What was his name?
Answer.
I cannot reveal that since he deserves to be protected.
She continued:
Dodi became very uncomfortable as he looked around the restaurant, he became even more and more agitated after he received a telephone call and began to look very hot and sweaty. He said the place was crawling with secret service people and they were watching us like hawks. He said, 'Come on Di we should leave' and he called the driver. The driver, Henri Paul, was definitely not drunk but he complained about strange feelings in his stomach and feeling a bit weird, he thought his drink had been spiked but said he felt well enough to drive We left with the bodyguard through the back entrance.

There were people in that tunnel, you know. I think they were secret service men. I have to explain. When I got into the car I had a dreadful sense of foreboding

but Dodi was making me laugh, reassuring me, holding my hand - he was always so affectionate.

Shortly after we entered the tunnel the driver started shouting hysterically. He kept putting his foot on the pedals, turning the wheel frantically and shouting 'No! No! I can't stop; watch out,' and he covered his face with his hands just before we crashed. I fell forward and Dodi tried to protect me before the impact.

Then we just lifted from our bodies and moved away. I know that I survived for a while after the crash but I was out of my body. I could see our bodies in the car and that's when I saw the men. They had black hoods right over their faces. They were all in black and I heard one of them say to another 'Well-done mate.' It was very dark in the tunnel.

Question
What about the bodyguard?
Answer
I do not believe this man lost his memory. I am sure he is now scared of his own shadow. He knows what happened and I never really trusted him. Not like Burrell, I will always stand by that man, he was my friend and there are many more letters from me, which he holds. He was always there for me. He knew what the Royal Family had done to me. I was isolated in that awful palace and Charles was so cold towards me. I was so unhappy I used to cut myself with a razor and cover up the wounds. I was crying out for love but the staff and family just ignored me. I was terrified to put on weight because the press watched my every move

and that's why I used to make myself sick after binge eating.

Life was a living nightmare with that cold family especially that horrible Prince Phillip, how I hated him. Dodi was the only man who really made me happy and they took that happiness away and they deprived me of my lovely boys and my life. I want the truth to be known. There are so many lies and cover-ups. This is what they are good at! If things don't suit them they have them changed.

Question
What are the dark forces at work in the palace, which the Queen mentioned to Burrell?
Answer
I don't really know it's all so secret. Everything I did and said was reported back to Charles, Prince Phillip or the Queen. The only friend I had was Sarah Ferguson. We use to have a laugh together. She was a lovely person and just look at her now. She's done so well and I'm glad for her. They turned on her as well when they knew we were close. I wish I had left her a big slice in my will. Prince Andrew is the best of the lot of them. He was always kind to me and treated me like a sister.

Question
There are rumours that your body is not in the tomb situated on the lake. Is this true?
Answer
I'm not in there. I'm buried with my Father.

Question

So you are not on the island?

Answer

No, I'm with my Father. I am furious with that brother of mine. He is just making money out of me that's why he wanted my body on the estate. (She becomes very agitated) Things are not as they appear.

Question

You obviously don't think much of your brother?

Answer

He's my brother so I suppose I must love him in a certain way but he was always a spoiled little brat and he's a womaniser and drinks too much. I remember when he was a young boy, if he couldn't get his own way he would stamp his feet, scream and go red in the face until he got what he wanted. I shall never forgive him! When I needed love and protection he wasn't there for me.

Question

Dodi's Father believes it was an assassination.

Answer

Of course he does because it is true. He wants to go to court and why not, he lost his lovely son-his own flesh and blood? He loved his son and he loved me. People don't know him. He's a lovely man - a very spiritual man and he wants the truth and the truth will come out. Although a lot of people claim they have contacted me in spirit, I have only come through this medium regarding the truth of the matter. I will state again that the crash was a set-up. They didn't want

Dodi and I to be happy, we were an embarrassment to the Royals.

Question
What happened to the baby?
Answer
Died instantly in the crash.

Question
But the pathologist claims there was nothing in your womb.
Answer
Well I was pregnant and I told Dodi's Father I was pregnant. It's all part of the cover-up and the lies.

Question
What was it like living in the palace?
Answer
I'm ashamed to talk about the palace. I was watched constantly by people and told what to do. I used to sneak down to the kitchens at night and eat for pure comfort. I was so depressed by the whole atmosphere and I always seemed to be alone, even though there were many people around. No one had any time for me and I could never venture outside because the press would be waiting. They were always spying on me. I hated the way I was living and never wanted to be the star I was made out to be. I was made to look like a downright snob and I wasn't like that at all. I was a very down to earth person. To be truthful, it was Charles who was the snob and at times a very cruel man.

Question
Did you hate Charles?
Answer

Yes, I did. After a while I had no feelings for him because he treated me so badly but I loved my boys and doesn't William look like me? He is a lovely natural boy but his Father is controlling him. I get the feeling he is turning my sons against me.

I was a good and loving Mother despite what anybody says. I'm sure Harry took drugs because he lacked love and affection and felt a little bit left out of things. He is a troubled soul who needs a mother.

The Royal Family has the habit of controlling things and people and how I hated that Prince Phillip; he made me go cold. I hated his eyes and he was such a crude man. Have you noticed how little people hear about Prince Phillip? He controls things but he hides in the background. He never liked me and I know he wanted me dead and out of the way. I know that Prince Charles was not responsible for my death; for all his faults he would never be party to such a thing!

Prince Phillip hated me so much and one day he flew in to a rage and raised his fist to me, I thought he was going to grab and shake me. He really hated me.

Question
What about your family?
Answer

I've told you what a spoilt brat, my brother is. It was always difficult trying to speak to him. I never really got on with my mother, she was very jealous because I was so close to my beloved Father. As for my sisters I have no feelings whatsoever. Sarah Ferguson was the person I shared secrets with and had such fun and I've told you what the Royals did to put and end to that source of happiness.

Question
How can you be so sure it was people in the palace who arranged the accident?
Answer
I wish I could give you absolute proof but I know the order came from high- up They wanted me out of the way. They didn't like me being with Dodi. You must believe this is me - Diana speaking. That car had been tampered with crossed wires or something under the bonnet. I could say so much but the medium is losing energy and I must go now. I would like you to come back, as I want to tell you more. Come tomorrow, please!'

*An ongoing police enquiry recently revealed that the car she travelled in on that fateful night, had been changed at the last minute.

Second Session

We returned the next day and once again the medium went into trance. Much of what we heard was a reiteration of the previous day's information. She claimed:

- **The car brakes or controls had been tampered with either before or in the tunnel.**
- **Points the finger at Prince Phillip as the man behind the crash**
- **Talks of her affection for her Butler, Burrell and claims he has more documents to reveal**
- **Had a sickening premonition on that fateful night as she entered the car that something was terribly wrong.**
- **Talks about staff at the palace who took drugs and held secret Gay and Lesbian parties**
- **Predicts that Charles will stand down and that William will become King of England**
- **Hated Camilla Parker-Bowles and believes that Charles will make a grave mistake in marrying her.**
- *Claims that her sons were very fond of Dodi and that they all got on well.*
- *Speaks about a coldness, which runs through the Royal Family in particular Phillip, Charles and Princess Ann, who she refers to as a little madam!*
- *Claims she was so unhappy and degraded by life in the palace that she tried to kill herself by taking an overdose. She lived in a state of deep insecurity and fear. Treated as if she didn't exist.*

- *Craved a normal family life and loved her work with the poor and the sick and the elderly.*

Throughout these sessions she was constantly persuading us that it really was her speaking through the medium. I am a journalist and have faithfully recorded to the best of my ability what took place over those two days. I find it very difficult to believe that this simple trance medium could have carried this sort of sensitive detail, since, I understand, she rarely reads or watches the television. This meeting took place on the 12th of January where Diana revealed that she injured herself. This fact was not officially published in the press until the 14th of February when some tapes had been sold to American television. There has been no substantial editing of this interview and no part of the above reflects any opinion I may hold. I have no agenda except that I fulfilled an assignment for which I was paid. I have no idea whether the above is true or otherwise - it was something I experienced and the reader must decide whether to accept or reject this information.

Alan Pemberton

A few weeks after this initial interview the medium posted an envelope to Rosemary Spencer which contained some hand written sheets of paper. The words were obviously taken down at great speed and were allegedly from Lady Diana again. The medium said that she had been compelled to sit for ages at her table whilst these words tumbled into her mind.

Diana

My heart must be set free, so that I can be at rest. I want to be left in peace - to be a free-spirit left in peace to continue my work in the spirit world.

I feel it is so degrading to know that people are still making money out of my name when I am no longer on the earth. I have already told you everything one needs to know about my life and death.

My life was hell and most of the time I was sad and lonely. Forget about me as the famous public figure moving in the twilight. I want the public to know the real truth about what went on behind closed doors. I know that I touched the hearts and souls of thousands of people when on earth. Now I want them to know the real Diana and what she really went through; about the coldness that I felt was directed at me in the palace; the great fear I had of Prince Phillip and how he belittled and threatened me.

My love is all for my children. I am still so much around them and am so proud of them.

Harry needs love and feels, at times, neglected. He rebels against people and feels hurt and angry. They should listen to him and realise that it is all a cry for help. He needs attention and I know he misses his mother's love. William is like me in the many ways; he is kind, loyal and loving and he will be a happy man with many admirers. He will become King of England one day and a fine King he will make!

You must believe this is Diana speaking - it really is me. So many people have wanted answers to unanswered questions and I intend to give them these answers.

Dodi was my life, my love and most of all my best friend. He was my soul mate and we were very much a serious item. We were meant to be together and he made my life worth living. He made me feel like a real woman and had lovely warmth about him. I found something magical about him that attracted people to him.

All I ask is that my name is laid to rest and I am allowed to continue my life in spirit. The whole affair is a mess and the only truth you will get will come from me. I want answers to the tragedy to come out. No if's and buts and no hush hush money payments to keep things quiet.

Dodi's father has the right to know the truth. He lost his son, his own flesh and blood and this is why I am coming through this medium to tell my story. I want this finished and the chapter closed; all this is hurting my sons deeply. I really want my sons to remember me as I was - the good times we shared together and how much love I had for them - they were my life!

I want the public to know my life in the palace was a living hell dominated by very high-up people. I was so lonely and had no one to confide in apart from my former butler. He was like a brother to me.

Those so-called high-up people don't want to believe

my story but I can assure you this is I, Diana, speaking from the other side! Palace life literally destroyed me!

In the world of spirit we live in harmony - it is the Kingdom of light, which shines all the time. There is no darkness except in the lower realms where the lost souls are.

I do not blame Charles for my death - he had nothing to do with it - but there was no love left between us and he was so cold towards me. I know he was emotionally wrecked when I died; a lot of it may be guilt.

I have to repeat that my death was not an accident - it was arranged to stop Dodi and myself being together. Yet our love has never died and we still go on together. His Father wants justice and the whole truth.

I have given all the details in a previous message through this medium. I just want to repeat that Dodi had received a phone call whilst at the Ritz and our lives were threatened. I shall never forget how frightened Dodi looked. He was sweating and anxious and that's why we left by the back entrance. He knew something was seriously wrong but comforted me by saying it was a hoax. He was in a great hurry to leave and when we were in the car his eyes were full of fear. He knew something was going on. This was no accident it was a set-up and the truth is now there for people to believe or ignore.

I stand by those people who cared for me - my pal Sarah Ferguson, Prince Andrew, and my former butler Paul Burrell - he always listened to my fears and worries and was a very dear friend.

Ends

A great deal of the second communication seems to repeat what is in the first. It is slightly less detailed but basically is desperately trying to make people see her side of things. In most great conspiracy cases, although the weight of evidence can be stacked as high as Everest, it rarely comes to a satisfactory conclusion. In most cases time takes the sting out of urgency and then evidence is contradicted to such an extent that's it difficult to know what to believe and that is the name of the game. The finger of justice rarely prods the guilty chest because it is always many steps removed from the person who gave the order.

End